Large Print Version Smart Retirement Budgeting

Proven Strategies for Maximizing Savings and Minimizing Expenses

June Dashlane

Plan 4 Everything Publishing

This book is dedicated to all the Budget Busters of the world.

book, without the consent of the author, illustrator, or publisher

Disclaimer Notice:

Please note the information contained within this document is for educational and entertainment purposes only. All effort has been executed to present accurate, up to date, reliable, and complete information. No warranties of any kind are declared or implied.

Readers acknowledge that the author is not engaged in the rendering of legal, financial, medical or, professional advice. The content within this book has been derived from various sources. Please consult a licensed professional before attempting any techniques outlined in this book.

By reading this document, the reader agrees that under no circumstances is the author responsible for any losses, direct or indirect, that are incurred as a result of the use of the information contained within this document, including, but not limited to, errors, omissions, or inaccuracies.

CONTENTS

INTRODUCTION

ARE YOU A WEALTH WASTER?

Recognize the importance of tracking small expenses.

Have you ever had an expense explosion? You reach the end of the month and review your expenses, only to find that the past month was nothing short of a spending avalanche. Our memories may fail us as we age, but that's no excuse for not remembering all the mindless purchases that led to this experience.

I realized that despite my best efforts, I still spent more money than I had intended. So, I kept track of my expenses for a month to see where my hard-earned money was going. To my surprise, I found that most of my expenses were small, seemingly insignificant purchases I made without a second thought. A cup of tea here, a magazine there, and before I knew it, I was spending a substantial amount on things I couldn't even remember buying.

These small expenses add up over time, draining my savings that I rely on for my golden years. So, I made some changes. I started bringing my own tea from home, borrowing magazines from the library, and avoiding impulse purchases. These small changes made a big impact on my finances, and I was able to save a substantial amount each month.

From that day on, I learned that it's not just the big expenses that waste money, but the small ones too. I became more mindful of my spending habits and made sure to keep track of every penny that went out of my pocket. With this newfound awareness, I was able to live a more financially stable and stress-free retirement.

As people, age, healthcare, and living costs continue to increase, while funds in retirement accounts continue to dwindle. Many seniors fear they won't be able to support themselves financially in their later years, especially if they didn't adequately save and prepare.

In this book, you'll discover ways to save money, regardless of your reason. The economy today requires people to be more conscientious about their finances. With the cost of everything rising, it's essential to find ways to save. From putting money into a retirement fund or savings account to finding hundreds of other ways to save, this book will show you how to be creative and learn about all the different options available to you.

Saving money is more than just putting a lump sum of cash aside. It's about finding savings in your everyday life through your choices and how you live. Rome wasn't built in a day, and neither will your bank account. But every penny saved is one more penny than before. Even if you can't save big, this book will show you how little savings can add up quickly.

It's never too late to start saving, regardless of your age. Set your mind that now is the time to build your future. Be encouraged and take the first step towards financial stability."

THE WATER POT ANALOGY

Think of your finances as a water pot. Every day, you fill it to the top with fresh, clean water, ready to quench your thirst. But, just like the water pot, your finances have leaks. Every day, you lose money through small expenses that add up.

WHAT HAPPENS THEN ?

By the end of the day, your water pot is empty, and so is your wallet. This happens to our finances unless we take control and plug the leaks. If we don't fix these leaks, we'll reach a point where we need to buy something important, but our financial pot will be empty.

The solution is simple: Start by plugging the biggest leaks first. Fixing just one big leak will keep your water and financial pots fuller for longer. Then, fix a few more leaks, and your financial pot will be full when you need it. So, take control of your finances today and plug the leaks to ensure a bright financial future.

THE NEST EGG ANALOGY

Think of your savings as a nest egg you've been carefully building over the years. Just as you would protect a real egg from cracking, you want to protect your nest egg from being depleted too quickly.

But like the water pot, your nest egg can also have "leaks" in the form of small, seemingly insignificant expenses that add up over time. These expenses can drain your nest egg faster than you'd like.

To keep your nest egg intact, you must plug the leaks by being mindful of your spending habits and making smart financial decisions. This might mean avoiding impulse purchases, cutting back on unnecessary expenses, or finding ways to reduce your monthly bills.

Doing this will ensure that your nest egg remains full and secure, giving you peace of mind and the financial security you need in retirement.

CHAPTER ONE

REALIZING YOUR CURRENT FINANCIAL SITUATION

As you near retirement or enter into it, it's essential to regularly reassess your financial situation to ensure you're on track to meet your long-term goals. By doing so, you can make any necessary adjustments to your financial plan and have peace of mind knowing that you're prepared for the future. In this chapter, we'll cover several steps you can take to reassess your financial situation, including creating a budget, tracking your spending, updating your retirement plan, identifying what matters to you, and setting achievable goals.

Creating a budget is the first step in understanding where your money is going and making informed decisions about your spending. By tracking your spending, you'll have a clear picture of how much you're spending each month and where your money is going. This information can help you identify areas where you may be overspending and make changes to reduce those expenses.

Updating your retirement plan is critical to ensuring a secure financial future. This may include reviewing your investments, updating your savings goals, and considering any changes to your lifestyle that may impact your financial plan.

Identifying what matters to you is also crucial in reassessing your financial situation. This could be paying off debt, traveling, or leaving a legacy for your loved ones. By knowing what matters to you, you can make sure that your financial plan aligns with your values and priorities.

Finally, setting achievable goals is essential to reassess your financial situation. This could include increasing your monthly savings, paying off debt, or creating an emergency fund. By setting achievable goals, you can take control of your financial future and ensure that you're on track to meet your long-term financial goals.

By taking these steps to reassess your financial situation, you can ensure that you're on track to meet your long-term goals and make any necessary adjustments to your financial plan. With a clear understanding of your spending, goals, and values, you'll have peace of mind knowing that you're prepared for life 2.0.

BUDGET

Everyone should create a budget. However, if you are trying to figure out how or are just not good with money, many businesses, such as H&R Block, offer free financial consulting to help you put a budget together. Knowing where you are spending your money is the best way to save. Unfortunately, in most cases, people have yet to learn where their money is going, and once they see it on paper, they are not only surprised but also eager to change their spending habits. If you are wondering where to start, go to Google and search for budgeting tips, and you will find plenty of free advice, including spreadsheets. Another great place is to try your bank's website and go to the loan application area. They should have some free budget sheets as well. Review your budget: Make sure you have an accurate and up-to-date understanding of your monthly income and expenses. This will help you determine if you're spending within your means and identify areas where you can make changes to save money.

TRACK YOUR SPENDING

Keep a record of your spending for a few months to better understand where your money is going. This will help you identify areas where you can cut back and change your spending habits.

UPDATE YOUR RETIREMENT PLAN

If you have a retirement plan in place, review it to ensure it's still relevant to your current financial situation and goals. Take into account any changes to your income, expenses, or other factors that may impact your retirement plan.

REVIEW YOUR INVESTMENTS

Take a close look at your investment portfolio and make sure it's aligned with your risk tolerance and long-term financial goals. Consider consulting with a financial advisor if you need help making investment decisions.

CONSIDER YOUR INSURANCE COVERAGE

Make sure you have adequate coverage for your needs, including health insurance, life, and long-term care insurance. Review your coverage regularly to make sure it's still adequate and cost-effective.

PLAN FOR LONG-TERM CARE

Consider your options for long-term care and make sure you have a plan for this eventuality. Long-term care insurance or government-funded programs, such as Medicare, may be options to consider.

CONSIDER YOUR ESTATE PLAN

Review your will, power of attorney, and other estate planning documents to make sure they reflect your current wishes and are up to date.

GET OUT OF DEBT

- Assess your debt and list all your debts, including the creditor, interest rate, and monthly payment amount.

- Shop for the best rates: Compare interest rates and terms from multiple lenders to find the best debt consolidation or refinance option.

- Consider the total cost: Pay attention to the total cost of the loan, including fees and closing costs, and not just the interest rate.

- Read the fine print: Carefully review the loan terms and conditions, including any fees or penalties, to avoid surprises later.

- Consider your credit score: A higher credit score may lead to lower interest rates and better terms, so improve your credit score before applying for a loan.

- Consider the length of the loan: Longer loan terms can reduce monthly payments, but they will also result in more interest paid over the life of the loan.

- Consider a secured loan: If you have collateral such as a home or a car, consider a secured loan, which may offer lower interest rates than an unsecured loan.

- Be careful with debt management companies: Be cautious when working with debt management companies, as some may charge high fees or engage in unethical practices.

- Seek professional advice: If you need clarification on debt consolidation or refinancing, consider speaking with a financial advisor or credit counselor for guidance.

- Create a plan for paying off debt: Once you have consolidated or refinanced your debt, create a plan for paying it off as quickly as possible to avoid future financial stress.

ALLOWANCE

Remember to give yourself an allowance for things you enjoy. Even if you are on a tight budget, buy something that you want, which could be as simple as buying a new shirt or grabbing lunch at your favorite café. If you do not allow this small "splurge," you could find yourself in the same position as if you were dieting. Total deprivation leads to overindulgence.

The whole idea of this book is to show you how to save money while simultaneously living an everyday life. What's the point of scrimping and saving to only live a miserable life? You can still spend money and be generous to others, even more so by being smart with money in other areas of your life.

WHAT MATTERS TO YOU

Make a list of the 10 most essential things in your life. Next, to each item, rank them in order of importance using numbers 1 through 10. The purpose of this exercise is to help you see the things you consider the most and least important and to provide you with a visual of why you need to save. Some examples of things a person might put on their list include a new home, car, memorable trip, artwork, starting a business, or paying off debts. Sometimes it pays to itemize how you are going to get those items. For example, if you go for a new home, you could use the home's equity to purchase a car. However, if you went for the car first, you would need help to get home. See what I mean? Sit down, itemize what you want, and then draw up a plan for achieving those results.

SETTING GOALS

Break your goals into short-term, intermediate-term, and long-term. Seeing your accomplishments is an excellent motivator to work hard at saving. If you set a short-term goal of saving for tickets to the symphony and reach that goal, you will be encouraged to keep saving for the intermediate and long-term goals.

BE REALISTIC

When saving money, make sure the goals you set for yourself are realistic. For example, if you are living on $50,000 a year, saving $20,000 would be nice, but it is very

unrealistic. Make your goals attainable, or you will never save.

HAVE FLEXIBILITY

Once you have set your goal for saving, realize that things can and will change. The secret is learning ways to be flexible. For example, if you save $150 a month when something unexpected happens, you may only be able to save $50 that month. This is fine as long as you focus on getting back on track.

INSURANCE

Shop around for insurance and work with a good agent that can provide information on discounts such as good student, multi-car discounts, etc. Some people think the insurance price is the same from one company to the next. However, prices can vary dramatically, and to ensure you get the best deal, you need to consider all your options. You can save enough from your insurance costs to pay for a decent end-of-year holiday.

ATTITUDE

Good money management is an acquired skill. As you save money, you need to have a positive attitude, which will often keep you and your family heading in the right direction. If you cannot save, then you probably will not. Be determined and stay optimistic about saving.

SELL YOUR STUFF

Go through your house and pull together all the items you no longer use. These can include small or large appliances, gardening tools, clothing, makeup, sporting equipment, or whatever you have, and then list them on eBay.

- Take the money earned from these sales and put it in your savings account, not to be touched.

- Determine the value: Research the market value of your items to determine the best price for them.

- Clean and organize: Clean and organize the items you want to sell so they're more attractive to buyers.

- Take good photos: Take good, clear photos of your items from multiple angles to showcase their condition and features.

- List online: List your items on online marketplaces such as eBay, Amazon, Facebook Marketplace, or Craigslist.

- Use social media: Utilize social media platforms such as Instagram or Facebook to reach a wider audience and advertise your items for sale.

- Offer multiple payment options: Offer various payment options such as cash, PayPal, or Venmo to make the transaction more convenient for the buyer.

- Price competitively: Price your items competitively, considering their condition, age, and market value.

- Be honest: Be honest about the condition of your items and disclose any defects or damage.

- Offer a warranty: Consider offering a warranty or return policy to build trust with potential buyers.

- Participate in community sales: Community sales, garage sales, or flea markets to reach a local audience and sell items in person.

TURN YOUR HOBBY INTO MONEY

Everyone has a skill – find yours and turn it into money. For example, if you have a talent for woodworking, start creating children's toys or charcuterie boards to sell. Perhaps you are social media savvy and could teach a class at your local community college. Find something you enjoy and sell it.

- Assess your skills and interests: Consider your skills and interests to determine what hobby could become profitable.

- Research the market: To determine your product or service demand and identify potential competitors.

- Create a business plan: Create a business plan that outlines your goals, target audience, marketing strategy, and financial projections.

- Build a following: Utilize social media and other online platforms to build a following and showcase your products or services.

- Network with others in the industry: Network with others to gain valuable insights, establish partnerships, and find potential customers.

- Offer a unique selling proposition: Offer a unique selling proposition that sets you apart from competitors and appeals to your target audience.

- Invest in equipment and supplies: Invest in the necessary equipment and supplies to produce your products or deliver your services.

- Price competitively: Price your products or services competitively, taking into account the costs of production and market demand.

- Continuously improve: Improve your products or services and stay up-to-date with industry trends to stay ahead of the competition.

- Seek professional advice from an accountant, attorney, or business coach to ensure you're on the right track and make informed decisions.

RECYCLE

Try a different type of recycling that will save you money. For example, have you ever received a nice gift that you like from someone but will never use? Rather than take it back to the store for an exchange, consider keeping it to give as a gift to someone else.

Another way to recycle is to look around your home. There are always things right in your home that can be used to make nice gift baskets – items you never use.

For example, the next time you purchase shower gel, where you buy one and get one free, keep one for yourself and set the other aside for future gift-giving. You will find hundreds of ideas, so be creative and consider things you purchased but have never used.

WHAT CAN I RECYCLE TO MAKE MONEY?

- Scrap metal: Scrap metal, including aluminum, copper, and steel, can be sold to recycling centers for cash.

- Electronic waste: Electronic waste, such as old cell phones, laptops, and televisions, can be sold to electronics recyclers for cash.

- Cardboard and paper: Cardboard boxes and paper products, such as newspapers and magazines, can be sold to recycling centers.

- Glass bottles and jars: Glass bottles and jars can be sold to recycling centers or redemption centers for cash.

- Plastic bottles and containers: Plastic bottles and containers can be sold to recycling centers or redemption centers for cash.

- Batteries: Used batteries can be sold to recycling centers for cash.

- Tires: Old tires can be sold to tire recycling facilities for cash.

- Car parts: Car parts, such as engines and transmissions, can be sold to auto recycling facilities for cash.

- Clothing and textiles: Clothing and textiles, including old clothes and linens, can be sold to secondhand stores or textile recyclers for cash.

- Ink and toner cartridges: Empty ink and toner cartridges can be sold to recycling centers for cash.

OVERDRAFT PROTECTION

Almost everyone has, at one point or another, bounced a check. Most banks charge $35 per returned check, which can quickly add to a lot of money if you are careful with your account.

If you have a savings account, consider adding overdraft protection to your checking account. Then, if you ever go into a negative balance, your savings will automatically cover the money. Most banks offer this service for free.

BANK ACCOUNTS

Make sure you work with a qualified banker to set up the "right" kind of account for your type of spending. Numerous options are specifically designed for people who write many checks versus those who do not. Check with your existing bank to ensure you have what you really need, and change banks if they are unwilling to work with you. In general, credit unions are good options. Their rates are typically lower, and you can find better options.

ORGANIZATION

You may be wondering what being organized has to do with saving money, but in reality, it has a lot to do with it. For example, if you miss a credit card due date by one day, you will be charged anywhere from a 15% to 25% penalty. The same would be valid for taxes. Missing one simple date can cost thousands. Therefore, it would help if you were organized so you know the exact dates your bills are due and keep all receipts, contracts, etc., orderly.

- Make a to-do list and prioritize

tasks.

- Use a planner to keep track of deadlines and appointments.

- Implement the "one touch rule," where you deal with an item only once.

- Keep your workspace clean and tidy.

- Use folders, binders, and labels to categorize and store information.

- Set aside designated times for checking and responding to emails.

- Use technology, such as task management apps, to your

advantage.

- Minimize clutter by regularly getting rid of items you no longer need.

- Delegate tasks to others when possible.

- Review and adjust your organizational system regularly to ensure it's still effective.

COORDINATE EFFORTS AND BE A TEAM

If you are married, make sure you and your spouse are working on the same agenda. What is the point if one is trying to save money while the other is busy spending? When you work as a team, you can encourage each other to keep on track with your saving.

LIFE SATISFACTION

Learn how to enjoy life and nature rather than possessions. The next time you feel like spending money, head to your local park, where you can enjoy the warm sun, green grass, and towering trees without spending a dime. Being happy in life is far better than buying item after item. Having inner peace is better than having a house filled with "Things." That does not mean you cannot enjoy some of the finer things in life; it just means learning to be happy with yourself and not "Things."

LIVE WITHIN YOUR MEANS

The quickest way to get in debt is to live beyond your means. Most people want more than they have, but life is not about spending money. Instead, be thankful for what you have and learn how to enjoy your financial position. This is where your budget will help identify the amount of money coming in against the amount of debt going out.

START A CHRISTMAS FUND

Many banks and financial institutions offer a Christmas Fund program. This is an excellent way to put aside money for your holiday shopping, so you only spend a bit.

With these programs, you do not miss the money; better yet, you have less stress around the holidays.

POCKET CHANGE CHA-CHING

Keep a jar or some container handy and drop in your change each time you come home. For example, put the change in your container every time you break a bill. You will be amazed at how quickly your money will build.

Chapter Two

Reassessing Spending Habits

Identifying and Eliminating Unnecessary Expenses

My clients, Jim and Susan, lived simple lives. They had always lived within their means, but as they entered retirement, they found themselves with more free time and money than they were used to. So they started to splurge on things they had always wanted but never could afford.

One day, Jim and Susan sat down to review their expenses and were shocked by how much they had been spending on things they didn't need. They had been treating themselves to expensive meals, luxury vacations, and high-end gadgets, but all the while, they were putting their retirement savings at risk. Finally, they realized they needed to catch up on the difference between wants and needs.

The couple committed to re-evaluating their spending habits and focusing on their actual needs. They started by listing their essential expenses, such as food, housing, and healthcare. They then made another list of their non-essential expenses, such as entertainment, travel, and gifts. They found that by reducing their spending on non-essential items, they could live a comfortable life and still have enough money to save for the future.

Jim and Susan learned a valuable lesson about the importance of distinguishing between wants and needs. They were grateful for the opportunity to take control of their finances and were proud of their steps to ensure that their retirement savings would last a lifetime. However, they realized that they could still enjoy life, but they needed to be mindful of spending and make choices aligned with their values and long-term goals.

We will now delve into how you can reduce expenses and make the most of your hard-earned money. The focus will be on avoiding temptation, having the right mindset, comparison shopping, understanding the difference between wants and needs, and managing subscriptions. This chapter aims to help you identify the areas in your spending that can be improved, so you can have more control over your finances and make more informed financial decisions. We will explore various strategies for making smart purchasing choices and discuss the importance of being mindful of your spending habits. Whether you're just starting out on your financial journey or have been managing your finances for years, this chapter will provide you with the insights and tools you need to make your money work for you.

PRUNING NONESSENTIAL EXPENSES

A nonessential expense is a cost that is not necessary for your basic survival or well-being. Here are some steps to help you determine what is a nonessential expense:

- Evaluate your income: Consider your monthly income and essential expenses, such as rent or mortgage, utilities, food, and transportation.

- Prioritize your expenses: List them, including nonessential ones, and rank them based on importance.

- Identify patterns: Look for ways in your spending, such as frequent dining out, subscriptions, or entertainment expenses.

- Evaluate your values: Consider which expenses align with your values and priorities and which may be less important.

- Create a budget: Create a budget that allocates funds for essential expenses and prioritizes spending on nonessential expenses.

- Track your spending: Track your spending for a few weeks or months to see where your money is going and identify areas for improvement.

- Make adjustments: Based on your spending analysis, make

adjustments to your budget by cutting back on nonessential expenses or finding ways to save on essential expenses.

Remember, nonessential expenses can vary from person to person and can change over time. Therefore, it's essential to reevaluate your spending regularly to ensure that your budget reflects your current needs and priorities.

FINANCIAL CONSULTING

Many financial companies and even churches offer outstanding classes on managing money. While some of these programs are free, others may have a nominal fee of around $35 to attend, but the money is well spent.

Another great option is consumer-counseling services. This is an excellent option for people in over their heads with debt. The counselors will work directly with your creditors to lower your balances and interest rates and establish workable payments that you can afford.

BREAK OLD HABITS

Take time to learn the various things that "trigger" your spending. For example, when you are depressed, lonely, sad, anxious, excited, whatever it may be, do you spend more?

Once you can identify these triggers, you can learn how to control them. For example, if you were just laid off from your job, although money is tight, you may have an overwhelming "need" to spend money.

You may notice that you head for the shops when you are bored. Knowing what affects you will help you discipline yourself and find other ways of comfort.

AVOID TEMPTATIONS

If you have a particular weakness, stay away from it. For example, if you love to gamble, stay out of the casinos. If you have a weakness for shoes, drive past your favorite shoe store. While avoiding temptation is hard, it is also necessary to save money. When you want to give in to your temptation, this is the time to use your "allowance."

THE RIGHT TIME TO SHOP

Studies have proven that when shopping while hungry, depressed, tired, and stressed, you buy more. So before you head to the grocery store, eat something. If you are upset or feeling a little blue, calm down or wait until you feel better before heading out to shop. As funny as it may sound, having a clear mind is essential when shopping and spending money.

THE RIGHT MINDSET

Having the right mindset when shopping can help you make smart and informed purchases, avoid impulse buying, and save money. Here are some tips for developing the right shopping mindset:

- Set a budget: Determine how much you can afford to spend and stick to it. This will help you avoid overspending and make informed purchasing decisions.

- Make a list: Write down the items you need to buy and stick to your list. This will help you avoid impulse purchases and stay focused on what you need to buy.

- Consider quality over quantity: Opt for high-quality items that will last rather than buying multiple cheaper items that need to be replaced frequently.

- Wait before making a purchase: If you need to decide whether you need an item, wait before making a purchase. The urge to buy will often pass, and you'll save money.

- Shop at sales: Look for sales and promotions to get the most for your money.

- Consider the total cost: Consider not just the upfront cost of an item but also the long-term cost, such as maintenance, repairs, or replacement.

- Shop with a purpose: Avoid shopping as entertainment or distraction. Shop with a goal and stay focused on what you need to buy.

By following these tips and developing the right shopping mindset, you can save money and make smart purchasing decisions.

COMPARISON SHOP

Comparison shopping can make a big difference in the price you pay. For example, you might be looking at a barbecue grill at one place for $350.00, and by making two more stops, find the same grill or one comparable for $300. In addition, consider the price of items assembled versus unassembled. For example, you might find the barbecue grill unassembled for $250. A couple of hours of "fun." assembling the grill is worth a $100 saving.

STOP COMPETING WITH THE JONES'

You do not have to compete with anyone. Be proud of what you have and who you are. If you can only afford an inexpensive sofa from a thrift store, find a nice throw, make a few pillows, and be proud and thankful. Competitiveness is a part of nature and, to a degree, healthy. However, when competition creates a buying war to see who can have the "best" when they have no business buying at all, then it becomes damaging. Stick to what you can afford regardless of what anyone else has or the pressure you might feel.

SALES CLERK COMPLIMENTS

Sales clerks are often paid on commission. Therefore, when you walk into a store and try on an expensive suit, you can be guaranteed you will hear several times over how wonderful you look, how great that suit fits you, etc. Because this is how the clerks make their money, they will say whatever it takes to make the sale. So you look good but do not allow yourself to be pressured into buying something beyond your means.

Know what you want and the price range you can work with, and stick with your own rules, not theirs.

CABLE AND STREAMING SERVICES

- Bundle services: Combine your cable, internet, and home phone services with one provider to get discounts. Negotiate with your cable company: Call your provider and ask for a better deal. Be willing to cancel if they don't offer a competitive package.

- Cut the cord: Consider canceling cable and opting for streaming services like Netflix, Hulu, and Amazon Prime Video.

- Choose a smaller cable package: Consider downgrading your cable package to only include the channels you regularly watch.

- Use multiple streaming services: Subscribe to multiple streaming services and alternate between them to avoid paying for too many at once.

- Take advantage of free trials: Most streaming services offer free trials, so you can test them before committing to a monthly subscription.

- Use a VPN: A virtual private network can help you access geo-restricted content and save money by switching your IP address to a different location with lower prices.

- Avoid premium channels:

Premium channels like HBO and Showtime can add up quickly, so consider skipping them or adding them only when needed.

WANTS VERSUS NEEDS

Make sure the thing you want to spend your money on is a "need." and not a "want." Sometimes this can seem like a fine gray line, but if you stick to the need list, you will spend less. I know one guy who used to say, "If I still want it in 3 months, then I'll get it".

9 times out of 10 in 3 months, he found that he or his children had forgotten about that particular want and therefore had saved themselves from wasting money on impulse buying. Determining the difference between a want and a

need can be challenging, but here are a few steps to help:

- Prioritize: Make a list of your expenses and prioritize them based on what is most important to you. Essential expenses like food, housing, and transportation are typically considered needs, while discretionary expenses like entertainment or eating out are considered wants.

- Consider your values: Reflect on what is important to you and what you value most. This can help you distinguish between what you genuinely need and want.

- Consider your goals: Consider your long-term financial

objectives and how your expenses fit into those goals. If an expense helps you achieve a goal, it may be more of a need.

- Evaluate your expenses: Take a closer look at each expense and consider whether it is necessary for your well-being or simply a desire.

- Practice mindfulness: Practice mindfulness when making purchases and resist impulse buys. Take time to consider each purchase and whether it is a need or want.

- Set a budget: Establishing a budget can help you keep track of your expenses and make it easier to identify wants versus needs.

- Reevaluate regularly: Regularly reevaluate your expenses and adjust your budget as needed. Your wants and needs may also change as your life and circumstances change.

PAY ON TIME

You are charged a late fee for every payment you pay late, which can range from $25 to $50 or more, depending on the company.

Therefore, if you made a $50 payment but it was paid late, something needed to be paid toward the debt. Instead, the entire $50 went toward an unnecessary fee. To avoid spending unnecessary money, mail your check-in time to avoid these fees.

MANAGE SUBSCRIPTIONS

- Keep a list: Make a list of all your subscriptions, including the name of the service, the cost, and the billing cycle.

- Review your subscription list regularly, at least once a quarter, to ensure you're only paying for services you need and use.

- Cancel unnecessary subscriptions: If you find a subscription you no longer need or use, cancel it to save money.

- Use a subscription management

tool: Use a subscription management tool, such as Trim or Billshark, to help you track and manage your subscriptions.

- Set alerts: Set alerts for when your subscriptions are due to renew, so you can decide whether to continue the service.

- Negotiate rates: If you have a subscription that you want to keep but find too expensive, try negotiating a lower rate with the provider.

- Take advantage of free trials: Before signing up for a subscription, consider taking advantage of any free trials to test the service first.

- Choose annual payments: If you sign up for a subscription, consider paying annually instead of monthly, as this can often result in a discount.

- Share subscriptions: If you have a subscription with multiple users, consider sharing it with family or friends to split the cost.

- Use cash-back websites: Use cash-back websites like Rakuten or Swagbucks to earn rewards for signing up for or renewing subscriptions.

REPAIR VERSUS REPLACE

Instead of spending $1,500 on that beautiful new couch, you might consider one of two options. If your couch frame is still reasonable, you might pay $600 to have it recovered or purchase a quality slipcover for $300. Redecorate in an instant with Slipcovers!

Your couch will look brand new for much less than it would replace.

Another example is if you have a lamp that you want to replace. Consider painting it and adding a new shade rather than spending money to buy a brand-new one. You may have a washer, dryer, or refrigerator that is running sluggish. Find out the cost of repair over that of purchasing a new one. Businesses offer fantastic paint jobs even if you have an appliance with the wrong color. With some creativity, you will be amazed at how much can be repaired, thus saving you money.

Plus, why not make some money from the same thing? Pretty up old lamps and sell them.

Chapter Three

Reduce

Expenditures

Strategies for saving money on groceries and household items

R etirement can be a time of financial uncertainty. Many retirees find themselves struggling to make ends meet on a fixed income. However, reducing expenditures on everyday necessities like groceries and household items can significantly impact your financial well-being. In this chapter, we'll explore practical strategies for cutting back on these expenses and putting more money back in your pocket.

One retired woman I coached, Betty, found that meal planning was a game-changer for her finances. Instead of making impulsive purchases at the grocery store or eating out, she began planning her meals and shopping for ingredients accordingly. Not only did this help her stick to a budget, but it also resulted in healthier, home-cooked meals that she thoroughly enjoyed.

We'll also discuss the benefits of buying in bulk, opting for store brands, and cooking at home, all of which can help you save money without sacrificing quality. And when it comes to gifts, we'll share some creative ideas for saving money while making your loved ones feel special. Whether you're on a tight budget or just looking to be more mindful about your spending, these strategies will help you reduce your expenditures and put more money back in your pocket.

MAKE A GROCERY BUDGET

Determine how much you want to spend on groceries and household items each month and stick to it. Refraining from impulse buys: Stick to a grocery list to avoid purchasing items not on the list

PLAN YOUR MEALS

Plan your meals for the week and make a grocery list based on the ingredients you need. This will help you avoid impulse purchases and waste. Although it will take some time initially, after you have planned a week's menu once, it will become much more manageable, and best of all, it will save you money. Knowing exactly what you will be making helps you to shop for foods that can be used more than once.As an example, if you are going to have spaghetti on Tuesday, you could buy bulk ground beef at a better price and then use the other half for tacos on Saturday. Another option would be buying round steak, where you fix Salisbury steak one night and then use the leftovers for breakfast hash a few days later. This will help you stretch meals and avoid last-minute or impulse buying.

USE A SHOPPING LIST

Stick to your shopping list and avoid buying items that aren't on it to save money.

Compare prices: Check the prices at different stores to find the best deals.

SHOP WITH A CASH BUDGET

Instead of using a credit card to avoid impulse purchases and overspending.

BUY SEASONALLY

Fruits and vegetables that are in season are often less expensive than out-of-season produce.

USE COUPONS

Okay, maybe you used to laugh as you watched people pull out their coupons at stores, but the truth is that using coupons can save you hundreds of dollars yearly. Coupons can be used at grocery stores, retail chains, and stores where the item is sold. In addition, some stores offer double coupon days, an extra bonus.

On average, you can save from 5% to 15% on a bill for $100 simply by presenting a coupon. Coupons are not just for food items; by scouring your local newspaper, you can find coupons for all sorts of merchandise.

Couponing can be an effective way to save money on your purchases. Here are some tips to help you get started:

- Organize your coupons: Keep them organized in a binder or

file folder, and categorize them by product or store.

- Plan your shopping trips: Before shopping, review your coupons and plan your trips based on the deals and sales available.

- Check for online coupons: In addition to physical coupons, many retailers offer coupons that can be used in-store or online.

- Combine coupons with sales: To maximize savings, combine coupons with sales and promotions.

- Know store policies: Familiarize yourself with coupon policies, including which coupons are

accepted and any restrictions,
such as the maximum redemption
limit per item.

- Be mindful of expiration dates:
Use coupons before expiration
and prioritize using ones expiring
soon.

- Be a smart shopper: Don't buy
items just because you have a
coupon. Make sure the item is
something you need and will use.

SHOP SALES

Wait for items you frequently use to go
on sale and stock up to save money.

BUY IN BULK

When items you use frequently are on sale, consider buying them in bulk to save money over the long term. Warehouse shopping saves a lot of money. You can always split large quantities even if you have a small family. The price of items in bulk is generally a great bargain. If you are single, you might go in with friends or family on bulk items.

Every town usually has a warehouse where you can buy bulk purchases.

Buying in bulk can save you money because it allows you to purchase larger items at a lower per-unit cost. Here's why:

- Lower unit price: When you buy items in bulk, the cost per unit is typically lower than when purchasing smaller quantities.

- Savings on packaging and shipping: Companies that sell in bulk often have lower packaging and shipping costs, resulting in lower consumer prices.

- Economies of scale: Companies that manufacture and distribute large quantities of products can benefit from economies of scale, resulting in lower consumer costs.

- Reduced waste: By purchasing in bulk, you can reduce the amount of packaging waste and minimize the frequency of trips to the store, potentially saving gas and time.

- Long-term savings: Buying items in bulk with a long shelf life, such as non-perishable food items, cleaning supplies, and personal care items, can result in long-term savings.

- However, it's essential to consider the cost of storage and the potential for waste if items go bad before they can be used, so it's essential only to buy what you will use in bulk.

BUY STORE BRAND ITEMS

These items are often just as good as name-brand items but cost less. Reconsidering brand loyalty: Try store brands or generic products to save money without sacrificing quality.

- Quality is similar: Store-brand items are often made by the same manufacturers as name-brand items and may be identical in terms of ingredients and quality.

- They are backed by a satisfaction guarantee: Many grocery stores offer a satisfaction guarantee for their store-brand items, meaning you can return them for a full refund if you are not satisfied.

- They are subject to the same regulations: Store-brand items must meet the same quality and safety standards as name-brand items and are subject to the same rules.

- They may have fewer frills:
  Store-brand items, such as fancy
  packaging or added ingredients,
  may have fewer frills, but
  the product quality is often
  unchanged.

- The ingredients may be the
  same: Store-brand items may
  contain the same ingredients as
  name-brand items, just packaged
  and marketed differently.

- They can be a smart choice:
  Choosing store-brand items can
  be a smart way to save
  money without sacrificing quality,
  especially for non-perishable
  items like pantry staples.

- The selection is expanding: As store brand items have become more popular, grocery stores have expanded their selection to include a wider range of products.

- Store brands may have different labels: Store items may be marketed under different labels within the same grocery store chain, but the quality and ingredients are often consistent.

- Taste tests show similar results: In many cases, taste tests have shown that store-brand items are just as good as, or even better than, their name-brand counterparts.

AVOID PRE-PACKAGED AND PROCESSED FOODS

These items are often more expensive than whole foods and contain fewer nutrients.

FREEZE FOODS

When you grocery shop, look for bargains on items that can be frozen. Most people do not even think about shredding block cheese and freezing it. Did you know that you can even freeze eggs? Give them a little room to expand. Then, when ready to use, set them out at room temperature. If you find apples on sale, make your own apple pies and freeze them or make applesauce.

Many food items can be frozen with no problem. Therefore, the next time you see a great bargain think about freezing. (Dairy products other than cheese do not generally freeze well).

SHOP AT DISCOUNT STORES

Stores like Aldi offer lower prices on groceries and household items.

GROW YOUR OWN FRUITS AND VEGETABLES

If you have a yard, consider planting a garden to save money on fresh produce. Regrowing produce: Grow produce from kitchen scraps to have fresh produce on hand.

COOK AT HOME

Eating out is often more expensive than cooking at home. Plan to cook most of your meals at home to save money.

REPURPOSING LEFTOVERS

Use leftovers from previous meals in new recipes to reduce food waste

USE A SLOW COOKER

Slow cookers are a great way to save money by using less expensive cuts of meat and making meals in bulk.

USE CLOTH BAGS AND CONTAINERS

Reduce waste and save money using cloth bags and containers instead of disposable ones.

CUT BACK ON ALCOHOL

Alcohol is often a significant expense. Consider cutting back or eliminating it to save money.

REDUCE ENERGY CONSUMPTION

Use energy-efficient appliances and light bulbs and turn off lights and electronics when they're not in use to reduce energy bills.

FIX INSTEAD OF REPLACE

When items break, try to fix them instead of replacing them to save money.

SHOP SECOND HAND

Find gently used items at thrift stores and yard sales to save money on household items.

USE PUBLIC TRANSPORTATION OR CARPOOL

Driving a car is often a significant expense. Consider using public transportation or carpooling to save money on transportation costs.

HOLIDAY GIFT GIVING

Here are some tips to help save money on holiday gift-giving:

- Make a budget: Make a budget for your holiday gift-giving and stick to it to avoid overspending.

- Shop early to take advantage of sales and promotions, and avoid last-minute price hikes.

- Consider homemade gifts: Make homemade gifts, such as baked goods, craft items, or photo gifts, which can be personal and cost-effective.

- Use coupons and discounts: Take advantage of coupons and discounts offered by retailers, both in-store and online, to save money on holiday gifts.

- Give experiences instead of things: Give the gift of experiences, such as tickets to a concert or show, a spa day, or a cooking class, which can be a unique and memorable gift.

- Re-gift: Consider re-gifting items that you no longer need or use, as long as they are still in good condition and appropriate for the recipient.

- Shop online to take advantage of

discounts and free shipping offers and avoid crowds and lines at physical stores.

- Choose thoughtful but inexpensive gifts: Choose thoughtful but inexpensive gifts, such as a photo album or a personalized piece of jewelry, to show appreciation without breaking the bank.

- Set a gift exchange limit: Consider setting a gift exchange limit with family and friends, such as a $10 or $20 limit, to reduce the cost of holiday gift giving.

- Volunteer: Consider giving back by volunteering your time and skills to a local charity or organization, which can be a meaningful and cost-effective way to celebrate the holiday season.

WRAPPING PAPER AND BOWS

Here are some tips to help you save money on wrapping paper and bows:

- Reuse old wrapping paper and bows: Reuse old wrapping paper and bows from previous years as long as they are still in good condition.

- Use alternative materials: Use alternative materials, such as newspaper, brown paper, and tissue paper, to wrap gifts. These materials are often less expensive than traditional wrapping paper and can be just as effective.

- Make your own bows: Make your own bows using ribbon or twine, which is often less expensive than pre-made bows.

- Buy wrapping paper and bows in bulk: Buy wrapping paper and bows in bulk, especially during holiday sales and clearance events, to save money in the long run.

- Shop at dollar stores and discount retailers: Shop at dollar stores and discount retailers, which often carry a selection of wrapping paper and bows at lower prices.

- Use reusable gift bags: Use reusable bags instead of wrapping paper and bows, as they can be used year after year and save you money in the long run.

- Cut wrapping paper to size: Cut paper sheets to size, rather than full sheets, to reduce waste and save money.

- Avoid over-packaging: Avoid over-packaging gifts, which can lead to more waste and higher costs.

REUSE

Here are some tips to help you save money by reusing things:

- Reuse containers, such as glass

jars, containers, and Tupperware, to store food and other items, rather than buy new containers each time.

- Use cloth instead of paper products, such as cloth napkins, towels, and tablecloths, which can be washed and reused.

- Repair broken items, such as clothing and electronics, rather than replacing them, to save money and reduce waste.

- Reuse gift bags and wrapping paper from previous years as long as they are still in good condition.

- Upcycle old items, such as furniture, clothing, and home

decor, to give them a new life and save money.

- Use rechargeable batteries instead of disposable batteries, as they can be recharged and used multiple times, reducing the need for constant replacements.

- Make your own cleaning products, such as all-purpose cleaners and laundry detergents, using ingredients like vinegar and baking soda, which are less expensive and better for the environment.

- Shop at thrift stores and garage sales to find used items that can be reused rather than buying new things at full price.

You can save money, reduce waste, and help protect the environment by reusing items.

DOLLAR STORES

Many years ago, dollar stores offered only off-brand products or poorly made merchandise. However, that has completely changed. Now you can walk into a dollar store and find the exact name-brand laundry soap, cleaning supplies, clothing, school supplies, everything for a fraction of the cost.

Where a store name-brand bottle of laundry detergent might cost $9.50 at a grocery store, you can find the identical product and size at the dollar store for $3.50. Check out your local dollar store and enjoy the mountains of savings.

DON'T GIVE UP THE GOOD STUFF

A misconception is that while trying to save money, you have to deal with sub-par merchandise, which is untrue. If you love fresh bread and pastries, visit a bakery thrift store. For your fresh fruits and vegetables, visit your local farmer's market. Try eBay or other auction sites to buy top-quality merchandise for a considerable discount. Watch for neighborhood garage sales or estate sales and auctions to find needed items. Even if you are looking for bargains to save money, you can still focus on quality.

CAR MAINTENANCE

- Regular oil changes: Change your oil every 3,000 to 6,000 miles or as the manufacturer recommends.

- Check tire pressure: Maintaining the proper tire pressure can improve fuel efficiency and extend the life of your tires.

- Rotate tires: Regular tire rotations can ensure even wear and extend the life of your tires.

- Replace air filters: Dirty air filters can reduce fuel efficiency and decrease engine performance. Replace them every 12,000 miles or as recommended by the manufacturer.

- Brake maintenance: Check your brakes regularly and have them serviced as needed to ensure they are working correctly.

- Battery maintenance: Check your battery regularly and have it cleaned or replaced as needed to ensure it starts your engine reliably.

- Fluid checks: Check your car's fluid levels, including engine oil, coolant, transmission fluid, power steering fluid, and brake fluid, regularly.

- Clean and wax your car: Regular washing and waxing can protect your car's paint and keep it looking new.

- Regular inspections: Take your car in for regular checks to catch and fix any potential problems before they become bigger.

- Drive sensibly: Avoid rapid acceleration, hard braking, and high speeds, as these can increase wear and tear on your car.

APPLIANCE MAINTENANCE

- Clean appliances regularly: Dust and debris can accumulate inside and affect their performance. Clean them regularly to ensure they are working efficiently.

- Check and clean coils and filters: Coils and filters in refrigerators, air conditioners, and other appliances should be checked and cleaned regularly to maximize their efficiency.

- Unplug appliances when not in use: This helps to conserve energy and prevent potential electrical fires.

- Use appliances correctly: Avoid overloading washing machines and dryers, and use the right detergent or cleaning products on appliances.

- Keep appliances level: Ensure appliances are level and stable to prevent wear and tear on their internal components.

- Replace old appliances: Older appliances are often less energy efficient, so replacing them with new, more efficient models can save money on energy bills in the long run.

- Schedule regular maintenance: Schedule regular check-ups and maintenance with a professional to keep appliances in good working order.

- Check and replace worn parts: Belts, hoses, and door gaskets can wear out over time and affect appliance performance. Check them regularly and replace them as needed.

- Keep appliances away from heat sources: Don't place appliances near heat sources like stoves or radiators, as this can cause them to overheat and break down.

- Use surge protectors: Surge protectors can help protect appliances from power surges, which can cause damage and shorten their lifespan.

HAIRCUTS

- Cut your own hair: With some practice and the right tools, you can save money by cutting your hair at home.

- Visit a barber school: Barber schools offer haircuts at a discounted price in exchange for the opportunity to practice on customers.

- Look for deals and coupons: Check local newspapers, websites, and social media for deals and coupons on haircuts.

- Try a home hair-cutting kit: You can purchase a home hair-cutting kit for a one-time cost and use it to cut your hair whenever needed.

- Visit a hairstylist who works from home: Some hair stylists work from home and may offer lower prices than a traditional salon.

- Join a hair salon membership program: Some salons offer memberships that provide discounts on haircuts and other services.

- Use a hair clipper instead of scissors: Hair clippers are cheaper and can be used for regular trims to keep your hair looking neat between haircuts.

- Ask for recommendations: Ask friends, family, or neighbors for advice on affordable hair stylists in your area.

- Avoid peak hours: Scheduling your haircuts during less busy times can lower prices, as stylists may offer discounts to fill open slots.

- Negotiate a lower price: Be bold and ask for a discount, especially if you are a regular customer or are paying cash.

SHOPPING FOR CLOTHES

There are many secrets relating to saving money on clothing. As a perfect example, buy the pieces separately rather than a matched suit for $550. This will save you about $100 to $150. Additionally, buy several pieces that can be mixed and matched, giving you six outfits out of four pieces. Make a list: Make a list of the items you need and stick to it while shopping to avoid impulse purchases.

- Shop sales: Look for sales and clearance events to get the best deals on clothing.

- Use coupons: Combine sales

with coupons to save even more money on your clothing purchases.

- Shop off-season: Buy seasonal clothing items when they are out of season to get the best deals.

- Buy basic items: Invest in high-quality basic items such as black pants, white shirts, and neutral-colored jackets, as these can be easily paired with different pieces.

- Shop second-hand: Second-hand stores, thrift stores, and online marketplaces such as eBay and Poshmark offer gently used clothing at a fraction of the cost.

- Sew your own clothes: Consider learning to sew your own clothing, as this can be a cost-effective way to get the items you need.

- Take care of your clothes: Properly care for your clothing and make repairs as needed to extend their lifespan and save money in the long run.

- Shop at discount stores: Discount stores such as T.J. Maxx and Marshalls offer brand-name clothing at a discounted price.

- Start with a color palette: Choose a color palette of neutral colors, such as black, white, gray, and navy, that can be easily mixed and matched.

- Invest in versatile pieces: Wear classic blazers, tailored pants, and basic tops that can be dressed up or down.

- Accessorize: Accessorizing with statement jewelry, scarves, and belts can add interest to basic outfits.

- Mix textures: Mix different textures, such as denim, leather, and silk, to create interest and depth in your outfits.

- Pay attention to fit: Make sure your clothes fit properly, as well-fitted clothing is key to creating a polished look.

- Choose quality over quantity: Rather than buying a lot of cheap, poorly made clothes, invest in a few high-quality pieces that will last.

- Add seasonal items: Mix in seasonal items, such as lightweight tops for summer or heavy coats for winter, to keep your wardrobe fresh.

- Keep it simple: A mix-and-match wardrobe works best when you stick to simple, classic styles and avoid trendy items that will quickly go out of style.

- Plan ahead: Consider the outfits you will need for different events and occasions to ensure your mix-and-match wardrobe is versatile.

TRENDY FASHION

Most people love to dress in the most up-to-date fashion, but you pay big bucks for those fashions. Instead, consider dressing with basics and then emphasizing them with trendy accessories. This will save you money on less expensive clothing while allowing you to dress it up.

PHONE

- Choose the right plan: Choose a cell phone plan that fits your usage habits, and consider switching to a less expensive option if your current plan is too costly.

- Use Wi-Fi: Take advantage of Wi-Fi whenever possible to avoid using cellular data.

- Avoid roaming charges: Turn off data roaming when traveling abroad to avoid costly roaming charges.

- Buy a refurbished phone: Consider purchasing a refurbished or used cell phone, as these can be significantly less expensive than brand-new models.

- Avoid insurance: Cell phone insurance can be expensive, so consider avoiding it if you are willing to take on the risk of damage or loss.

- Reduce screen time: The longer you use your cell phone, the more battery and data you consume. Reduce screen time to save on both.

- Use an app to track usage: Use an app to track your data and voice usage and make adjustments to your plan if needed.

- Take advantage of promotions: Look for promotions and discounts offered by cell phone carriers, as these can save you money on your monthly bill.

- Buy an unlocked phone: Buy an

unlocked cell phone and bring it to a carrier that offers prepaid or pay-as-you-go plans, as these can be less expensive than traditional plans.

- Keep your phone longer: Consider keeping your phone longer, rather than upgrading to the latest model, to save money on your cell phone expenses.

CONSOLIDATE ERRANDS

To save gas, organize your day of errands, so you get as much done in an organized manner as possible. Stay in the same geographical area and hit as many of your errands in that area as possible to avoid excessive driving.

Save time: Consolidating errands into one trip can save you time compared to making multiple trips.

- Reduce fuel costs: Making one trip for all your errands instead of multiple trips can reduce fuel costs and save you money on gas.

- Improve planning: Consolidating errands can help you plan more effectively and prioritize your tasks, allowing you to get more done in less time.

- Decrease wear and tear on your vehicle: Making fewer trips can decrease wear and tear on your car, helping you save money on maintenance and repairs.

- Better use of your time: By consolidating errands, you can use your time more efficiently and avoid wasting time sitting in traffic or waiting in line.

- Improved safety: By making fewer trips, you can reduce your overall exposure to road hazards and improve your safety.

- Reduce stress: Consolidating errands can help reduce the stress of rushing from one task to the next, allowing you to relax and enjoy your free time.

- Improved environmental impact: Consolidating errands can reduce your carbon footprint by decreasing the time you spend on the road and decreasing air pollution.

- Better organization: Consolidating errands can help you stay organized and keep track of your to-do list, making you more productive and efficient.

- Increased savings: By consolidating errands, you can save money on fuel, time, and wear and tear on your vehicle, leading to increased overall savings.

SHOP ONLINE

Many online businesses offer great bargains and, in some cases, free shipping. Since the Internet is such a competitive market, you can usually find fantastic deals. In addition, many of your favorite businesses where you shop in person have websites that offer even more significant savings. Bookstores like Amazon.com will sell up to 70% off the original price. Overstock.com is another online business that sells closeout items for fantastic bargains.

CONSIGNMENT SHOPS

Rather than throw out or sell slightly worn clothing or other household items in a garage sale, consider selling them through a consignment shop. You will get a better price for your items, and consignment shops always look for quality merchandise.

- Research: Before shopping, research consignment stores in your area and their reputation for quality and selection.

- Shop regularly: Consignment stores typically receive new merchandise regularly, so it's best to visit often to see what's available.

- Know your size and style: Be familiar with your size and preferred styles, as consignment stores may have a limited selection or may not carry your size.

- Scrutinize items: When shopping at a consignment store, carefully inspect each item for any damages, stains, or signs of wear.

- Check for authenticity: If you're buying luxury or designer items, check for authenticity to ensure you're getting what you paid for.

- Negotiate the price: Feel free to negotiate the price of items, as some consignment stores may be willing to lower their prices.

- Check for sales and promotions: Many consignment stores offer sales and promotions, so keep an eye out for discounts or special deals.

- Know the store's return policy: Before purchasing an item, familiarize yourself with the store's return policy if you need to return it.

- Shop with a list: Make a list of items you need and stick to it, as shopping at a consignment store can be overwhelming with the large selection of items.

- Be patient: Consignment shopping can be time-consuming, so be patient and take your time to find the right items at the right price.

BE A MALL WALKER – NOT A SHOPPER

Stay away from shopping malls. High-dollar shopping malls have expensive overheads designed to sell, sell, sell. As a result, prices are generally higher, and in most cases, people walk out with more than they anticipated buying. It is better to shop at stand-alone shops or on the Internet.

CAR SHOPPING

- Shop around for the best price. While you may focus on that "perfect" car and want it now, you could save yourself a lot of money by waiting and looking around. In addition, check out other states.

- If you live within a few hours' drive from other cities, check out the price difference. The five hours it takes to drive may be worth the money saved.

- Research before you buy: Compare different models and prices to find the best deal.

- Buy used: Buying a used car can be more cost-effective, as used cars are often priced lower than new ones.

- Consider financing options: Shop around for the best financing options, such as a low-interest loan, and compare the cost of financing with cash and leasing options.

- Negotiate the price: Feel free

to negotiate the cost of the car, including the sale price, financing terms, and any extras or upgrades.

- Get a pre-purchase inspection: Before buying a used car, inspect it by a trusted mechanic to identify any potential problems.

- Avoid extended warranties: Extended warranties may seem like a good idea, but they can be expensive and offer limited coverage.

- Avoid add-ons: Salespeople may try to sell you additional features or services, but many of these add-ons can be expensive and not worth the cost.

- Consider public transportation: Before buying a car, consider whether public transportation or car-sharing services would meet your transportation needs and save money.

- Maintenance and fuel costs: Consider the ongoing costs of owning a car, including maintenance, fuel, insurance, and taxes, when making your decision.

- Buy at the right time: Timing can also play a role in saving money on a car purchase. Consider buying at the end of the month, quarter, or year when dealers may be more willing to negotiate.

CHECK RECEIPTS AND STATEMENTS

If you were to check your grocery or store receipt, approximately 50% of the time, you would find an overcharge. This happens all the time, and in some cases, the charge can be substantial. The same applies to credit card statements, bank statements, phone bills, etc. So again, check the detail because it is common to find errors. These mistakes can easily be corrected simply by asking for and providing a copy of the receipt or statement.

DINING OUT

Eating out can be expensive. So rather than stop eating out, cut back and look for options of two-for-one. Restaurants of all calibers offer weekly specials, and if you check your Sunday paper, you can often find special bargains. You might even think about signing up as a Mystery Shopper on the Internet, where you can eat at fine restaurants for free or at a huge discount just for writing a report on the food, service, and cleanliness

SEASONAL BUYS

One to three days after a holiday, stores mark their holiday items from 50% to 75% off. This is an ideal way to stock up on next year's Christmas or Halloween decorations. This is true for stores that sell seasonal clothing as well. For example, shopping for jackets or sweaters in the summer will provide you with great deals.

CHAPTER FOUR

REBALANCING YOUR RETIREMENT INCOME

MAKING THE MOST OF YOUR SAVINGS AND INVESTMENTS

A few years ago, I worked with a retired man named John, who had always been responsible with his finances. He had worked hard his entire life and had saved enough money to live comfortably in retirement. However, as he got older, John started worrying about whether his retirement income would last as long as needed.

One day, John met with a financial advisor who helped him understand the importance of rebalancing his retirement income. The advisor explained that as John's investments grew, some of his assets might become over-weighted and could put his retirement savings at risk. John learned that rebalancing involved regularly adjusting his investment portfolio to ensure that his assets were diversified and aligned with his risk tolerance.

John was a quick learner, and he took the advice to heart. He began to review his portfolio regularly and made minor adjustments to ensure that his investments were in balance. He also started to take advantage of other opportunities to make the most of his savings, such as investing in a high-yield savings account and using tax-advantaged retirement accounts like IRAs.

As a result of his efforts, John could maintain a steady stream of retirement income for many years. As a result, he never had to worry about running out of money, and he could enjoy his golden years without stress. John was grateful for the knowledge and was proud of the steps taken to make the most of his savings and investments. He learned that taking control of his finances in retirement was possible and that with a little effort, he could ensure that his retirement income would last a lifetime.

Rebalancing your retirement income is a crucial step in ensuring the long-term sustainability of your savings and investments. This involves periodically reviewing your portfolio and adjusting it so that your investments align with your goals and risk tolerance. By doing so, you can avoid having too much exposure to any one asset class and reduce the risk of significant losses. Rebalancing allows you to take advantage of market opportunities and maintain a diversified portfolio. Additionally, it helps you maintain a consistent allocation of assets, ensuring that your retirement income is distributed evenly and allowing you to make the most of your savings and investments. To succeed in rebalancing, it is important to clearly understand your investment goals, regularly monitor your portfolio, and work with a financial advisor to make informed decisions.

MAKE ANNUAL PAYMENTS WHEN APPLICABLE

Making annual payments instead of monthly payments can save money in several ways:

- Discounts: Some companies offer discounts for annual payments, as it reduces administrative costs and provides a guaranteed income for the year.

- No monthly processing fees:

Monthly payments often come with processing fees, which can add up over time. Annual payments can eliminate these fees and save you money in the long run.

- Lower interest rates: Some loans, such as personal or car loans, may offer lower interest rates for those who opt to make annual payments instead of monthly payments.

- Avoid late fees: Making annual payments eliminates the risk of missing monthly payments and incurring late fees.

- Budgeting: Making an annual

payment can make it easier to budget and plan for the year ahead, eliminating the need to make monthly payments.

- Making an annual payment can provide peace of mind, knowing that many of your yearly expenses have been taken care of.

Making annual payments may only sometimes be the best option, as it requires a larger upfront payment. Therefore, it's important to consider your financial situation and budget before making the decision to make annual payments. If you need more clarification, consult a financial advisor for personalized advice.

START A SIDE HUSTLE

To determine the best side hustle for you, consider the following factors:

- Skills and interests: Identify your skills, interests, and passions, and think about how you can turn those into a profitable side hustle.

- Schedule and availability: Consider your existing schedule and how much time you are willing to dedicate to your side hustle.

- Income potential: Research different side hustles to determine which ones have the most income potential and align with your skills and interests.

- Start-up costs: Consider any

start-up costs involved in each side hustle and determine feasible ones.

- Location: Consider if the location is a factor for the side hustle you choose, such as if it requires a physical presence or can be done remotely.

- Market demand: Research the need for the products or services you are considering offering and determine if there is a market for your side hustle.

- Network: Utilize your existing network, such as friends, family, and professional contacts, to see if they have any experience or advice on your potential side hustle.

Remember, the best side hustle for you combines your skills and interests with a high income potential and manageable start-up costs. You may have to try several side hustles before finding the right one, so feel free to experiment and make adjustments along the way

RE SELL CLOTHING

Here are some tips to help you make money from reselling thrift stores and clearance finds:

- Research the market: Research the need to find out what items are in demand and what they are selling for to maximize your profits.

- Shop at thrift stores and clearance sales: Shop at thrift stores and clearance sales to find items priced lower than their market value, which you can then resell for a profit.

- Look for unique and high-value items: Look for unique and high-value items, such as designer clothing, vintage items, and collectibles, which can be resold for a higher profit margin.

- Check for brand names and quality: Check for brand names and quality when shopping, as these can increase the value of the item and help you sell it for a higher price.

- Clean and repair items: Clean and repair items before selling them to improve their condition and increase their value.

- Price items competitively: Price items competitively, based on market demand and their condition, to attract buyers and maximize your profits.

- Use online marketplaces: Use online marketplaces, such as eBay, Amazon, and Facebook Marketplace, to reach a wider audience and sell your items to people worldwide.

- Offer free shipping: Offer free shipping to attract buyers and increase the visibility of your listings.

- Take clear, detailed photos: Take clear, detailed photos of your items to showcase their condition and highlight their best features.

- Be professional and responsive: Be professional and responsive to your buyers, answering any questions and addressing any concerns they may have to improve your customer satisfaction and increase your chances of repeat business.

Following these tips, you can make money from reselling thrift stores and clearance finds and turn your passion for shopping into a profitable side hustle.

PATIENCE

Be patient when it comes to saving. This means that you need to accept that it will take time to save and good planning. Be patient and remember that just because you want something, do not rush to buy to satisfy your urge. Instead, wait for sales to get the best price, which in turn will save you money.

MAKE THE MOST OF SOCIAL SECURITY

Maximize your Social Security benefits by delaying benefits until age 70, if possible.

- Increased monthly benefits: Your monthly benefits increase by approximately 8% for each year you delay taking benefits between your full retirement age and age 70.

- Larger lifetime benefits: By delaying benefits, you'll receive larger monthly benefits for a longer period of time, which can provide a higher lifetime benefit.

- Increased financial security: Delaying benefits can provide increased financial security in retirement, particularly for those with a longer lifespan.

- Reduced reliance on savings: By maximizing your Social Security benefits, you may be able to reduce your reliance on other savings and investments, which can help to preserve your nest egg.

- Increased flexibility: Delaying benefits can provide increased flexibility in retirement, as you can choose to take benefits at a later date if needed.

CONSIDER A PART-TIME JOB

Working part-time can provide additional income and help keep you active and engaged.

- Additional income: The most obvious benefit of working a part-time job in retirement is the additional income it can provide.

This can help to supplement your retirement income and reduce the amount of money you need to withdraw from your savings and investments.

- Stay active and engaged: Working a part-time job can help keep you active and engaged, both physically and mentally, which can help to maximize your overall well-being.

- Sense of purpose: A part-time job can provide a sense of purpose and fulfillment, helping to counteract feelings of boredom and loneliness that can sometimes accompany retirement.

- Opportunities to learn: Working a part-time job can provide opportunities to learn new skills and knowledge, which can be valuable in both personal and professional contexts.

- Social interaction: Working a part-time job can provide opportunities for social interaction and the development of new relationships, which can be beneficial for mental and emotional health.

- Potential to delay tapping into retirement savings: The additional income from a part-time job can allow you to delay tapping into your retirement savings, which can help to preserve your nest egg for later in life.

- Increased financial security: By supplementing your retirement income with a part-time job, you can increase your overall financial security, helping to ensure you have the resources you need to enjoy your retirement to the fullest.

RENT OUT A ROOM

If you have extra space in your home, consider renting it out to generate additional income.

MAKE GIFTS FOR FAMILY MEMBERS

Consider making gifts to family members while you're still alive, which can reduce the size of your estate and potentially lower estate taxes.

TAKE ADVANTAGE OF A REVERSE MORTGAGE

If you have significant equity in your home, a reverse mortgage can provide a source of income.

CONSIDER ANNUITIES AND DIVIDEND STOCKS

An annuity can provide a guaranteed source of income in retirement.

Consider investing in dividend-paying stocks to generate a steady stream of income.

PLAN FOR LONG-TERM CARE

Plan for the possibility of needing long-term care in the future, as these expenses can be significant.

TAKE ADVANTAGE OF TAX BREAKS

Look for tax breaks and deductions for retirees, such as the senior citizens' tax credit.

MAXIMIZE PENSIONS

If you have a pension, make sure to maximize your benefits by choosing the best payout option.

BE MINDFUL OF INFLATION

Plan for inflation and its impact on your retirement income and expenses.

TAKE ADVANTAGE OF SENIOR DISCOUNTS

Many businesses offer discounts to seniors, so be sure to take advantage of these savings.

MAINTAIN AN EMERGENCY FUND

Keep an emergency fund to cover unexpected expenses and protect your retirement income.

STAY INFORMED AND ENGAGED

Stay informed about changes to retirement income and benefits, such as Social Security and pension changes.

Regularly review your investment portfolio to ensure it remains aligned with your investment goals and adjust it as needed.

CHAPTER FIVE

REDUCING HOUSING COSTS

MAKING YOUR HOME WORK: OPTIONS FOR DOWNSIZING OR RENTING

Once upon a time, a retired couple named Jack and Diane lived in the same spacious three-bedroom house for over 30 years. However, as they both entered their golden years, they found that maintaining the large home was becoming a burden on their fixed income. They needed help to keep up with property taxes, utility bills, and other maintenance costs.

One day, Jack and Diane sat down and talked about their options. They knew they had to do something to reduce their housing costs, but they didn't want to leave their beloved home. That's when they came up with an idea. They decided to turn one of their unused bedrooms into a rental space and rent it out to a young professional. The extra income would help cover some of their expenses, and they could use the opportunity to make new friends.

However, the couple soon realized that having a tenant meant additional responsibilities, like ensuring the space was kept in good condition and making sure their privacy wasn't compromised. So after a few months, Jack and Diane decided that this solution wasn't for them and started exploring other options.

That's when they discovered the concept of downsizing. They sold their large home and moved into a smaller, more manageable condo. They could use the sale proceeds to pay off their debt, reduce their monthly expenses, and still have enough money for travel and other activities they enjoy.

In the end, Jack and Diane were happy with their decision to downsize. They were able to live a comfortable life without the stress of maintaining a large home, and they were able to enjoy their retirement to the fullest.

In addition, they learned that reducing housing costs is possible with creativity and that there are many options for retirees looking to do the same.

Reducing housing costs is important for many people, especially in retirement, when the goal is to maximize one's savings and minimize expenses. Unfortunately, owning a home can be expensive, and with rising property values and taxes, it is becoming increasingly challenging to keep housing costs under control. This chapter will explore ways to do your homework for you, including ways to reduce housing costs and options for downsizing or renting. Whether you are looking to save money, simplify your life, or make the most of your retirement years, I will provide practical tips and strategies to help you achieve your goals. We will also examine the pros and cons of downsizing or renting and help you determine the best option for your needs and budget. By exploring these strategies, you can take control of your housing costs and make the most of your retirement years.

MORTGAGE PAYMENT

Paying one additional mortgage payment each year, whether in a lump sum or monthly

increments, can lower a 30-year loan to 18 years. If you pay more than one extra, the number of years will decrease even more. Since this additional payment will be applied only to the principal and not the interest, you end up saving thousands and thousands of dollars once the home is paid off. If you are budget-conscious, home equity loans will provide even more significant savings.

PROPER MAINTENANCE

Purchase an annual home warranty policy. These policies can run from $350 to $500 a year and offer valuable options. The way most of these policies work is that if you have something break, such as your garage door, dishwasher, air conditioner, etc.,

For a minimal fee, usually $50 to $100, a serviceperson will come to your home to fix the item. Best of all, if you have five things broken and the same serviceperson is qualified to fix all of them, you are still charged the $50 to $100 fee once, not five times. For your automobile, consider purchasing an extended warranty. If you ever need either of these policies, they will save you tremendous value.

ANNUAL HOME MAINTENANCE

Here is an annual home maintenance checklist to help you keep your home in good condition:

Spring:

- Clean gutters and downspouts

- Inspect roof and chimney for damage

- Check for air leaks around windows and doors, and seal as

necessary

- Test smoke detectors and carbon monoxide detectors

- Check and clean HVAC filters

- Service air conditioning unit

- Inspect the deck and patio for any damage or wear

- Clean the exterior of the home, including windows, siding, and trim

- Paint and maintain siding: Regularly paint and maintain the exterior of your home, especially the siding, to protect it from the elements and keep it looking good.

Summer:

- Inspect and repair any cracks or damage to driveways and walkways

- Check and repair any leaks in plumbing and fixtures

- Clean and service any outdoor grills or firepits

- Trim trees and shrubs

- Check for and treat any pests or insect infestations

Fall:

- Service heating unit

- Check for and repair any leaks in the roof or around the windows

- Insulate pipes and add weather stripping to windows and doors

- Clean chimney and fireplace

- Store outdoor furniture and grilling equipment

- Prepare garden beds for winter and cover them with mulch

Winter:

- Check for and repair any damage from ice

- and snow

- Clean gutters and downspouts

- Keep sidewalks and driveways clear of ice and snow

- Inspect and repair any damage to the roof and chimney

- Check and repair any leaks in pipes

- Check and replace batteries in smoke and carbon monoxide detectors

- Inspect electrical wiring: Check your electrical wiring and outlets for any signs of damage or fraying.

Note: This is a general annual home maintenance checklist, and may not cover all potential issues specific to your home. It's always a good idea to consult a professional if you have any concerns or questions about the maintenance and repair of your home.

INSULATION

The average home wastes hundreds of dollars every year due to improper insulation. Make sure no drafts are coming from your window, door, or fireplace. Ensure your home has the appropriate level of insulation, which will make a HUGE difference in your utility bill.

DOWNSIZING

Downsizing for a retired person can have several benefits, including:

- Lower cost of living: A smaller home typically means lower monthly expenses for utilities, taxes, and maintenance.

- Increased financial security: Downsizing can free up money for other expenses or investments, providing financial security in retirement.

- Improved health and wellness: A smaller home is often easier to maintain, reducing home upkeep's physical and mental strain.

- Increased mobility: A smaller home can be easier to navigate and access, especially for someone with mobility issues.

- Reduced clutter: Downsizing

helps retirees simplify their living space, reducing clutter and promoting a more organized lifestyle.

- More time for activities and travel: With a smaller home, retirees have more time and energy to pursue hobbies, travel, or volunteer.

- More opportunities for community involvement: Downsizing to a smaller home or a community with amenities designed explicitly for retirees can provide opportunities for social interaction and community involvement.

Note: The benefits of downsizing may vary depending on an individual's unique circumstances and priorities. It's always a good idea to consult a professional, such as a financial advisor or real estate agent, before making any significant life changes.

UTILITIES

Set up some rules in your home, such as turning lights off when leaving the room, having only a parent adjust the air or heat, and leaving the doors or windows open when letting either cold or hot air into the house. Utilities are expensive, and a great money saver is to monitor how they are used in your home. Another great idea is the investment of buying an energy-efficient hot water heater. If you cannot afford one, lower the setting, so you are not heating water so hot. The hotter the setting, the more energy is used.

RENTING OUT A ROOM

If you have extra space, consider renting a room to a tenant to generate additional income.

Here are some tips for renting out a room in your home

- Legal compliance: Check local laws and regulations regarding short-term rentals.

- Define the rules: Set clear rules for the tenant regarding quiet hours, shared spaces, and guest policies.

- Screen tenants: Thoroughly vet potential tenants with

background and credit checks to ensure a good fit.

- Set a fair price: Research the market to determine a reasonable rental price for your area and the amenities offered.

- Advertise effectively: Use online platforms such as Airbnb or VRBO to reach a broad audience and take high-quality photos to showcase your space.

- Keep the space clean and well-maintained: Regular cleaning and repairs can help attract and retain tenants.

- Provide basic amenities: Make sure the room is fully furnished and equipped with bedding, towels, and toiletries.

- Keep good records: Keep accurate records of rent payments and expenses for tax purposes.

- Communicate openly: Maintain open and clear communication with your tenant to resolve any issues.

RELOCATING

Research areas with lower housing costs and consider moving to a location with a lower cost of living. The following are the top 10 for Retirees.

- Lubbock, Texas

- Memphis, Tennessee

- Wichita, Kansas

- Tulsa, Oklahoma

- Knoxville, Tennessee

- Dayton, Ohio

- Buffalo, New York

- Grand Rapids, Michigan

- Oklahoma City, Oklahoma

- Louisville, Kentucky

RENTING A MOBILE HOME OR RV

Mobile homes and RVs can be more affordable than traditional homes or apartments. Renting a manufactured home or recreational vehicle (RV) can be a cost-effective housing option for retirees, especially if they are looking for a low-maintenance, mobile lifestyle. Mobile homes are often less expensive than traditional homes and can provide a more affordable housing option for seniors. Many manufactured home communities also offer amenities and activities specifically designed for seniors, such as swimming pools, fitness centers, and community centers. RVs offer even more mobility and freedom, allowing retirees to travel and explore new Destinations.

SHARING HOUSING COSTS

Consider sharing a home or apartment with a roommate or family member to split the cost of rent and utilities.

NEGOTIATING RENT

If you have been a good tenant, try negotiating your rent with your landlord to see if they can offer a lower rate. Offer to do maintenance or, assist with showings in an apartment complex.

LANDSCAPING

If you are considering creating a lovely flower garden area, shopping for plants, even on sale, can be expensive. Before you go out and start spending:

- Look around to see if you have other plants that can be split from your flowers.

- Compare prices before you go.

- Check out this Outdoor Decor online shopping center to get an idea of the prices before you venture out.

Additionally, if you have a good relationship with any of your neighbors, ask them if they have any plants you could use as a starter.

Another great idea is to buy a lawnmower the next time you are in the market and purchase one that mulches leaves. This way, you can use the mulch you make rather than buy mulch for your flowerbeds yearly.

Here are some tips to help you save money on landscaping:

- Plan your landscape: Plan your landscape carefully, considering the size of your yard, the amount of sunlight and shade, and the plants and features you want to include. This can help you avoid costly mistakes and ensure you get the most value for your money.

- Do it yourself: Consider doing some or all of the landscaping work, such as planting, mulching, and pruning. This can save you money on labor costs and also allow you to be more hands-on with your landscape design.

- Choose low-maintenance plants: Choose low-maintenance plants, such as native species, that require little watering, fertilizing, and pruning, saving you money on maintenance costs.

- Use drought-tolerant plants: Use drought-tolerant plants, which can save you money on watering costs and help conserve water.

- Use mulch: Use mulch, such as wood chips, to conserve water and reduce the need for frequent watering.

- Choose functional features: Choose functional features, such as pathways and retaining walls, that serve a practical purpose and add to your landscape's aesthetic.

- Buy plants and materials in bulk: Buy plants and materials in bulk, such as mulch, compost, and fertilizer, which can save you money and reduce waste.

- Reuse old materials: Reuse old materials, such as stones and bricks, to create unique and cost-effective features in your landscape.

By following these tips, you can save money on landscaping and create a beautiful outdoor space that you can enjoy for years.

HEATING AND COOLING

Ensure vents in rooms are not being used or the garage is closed. Many people tend to try to heat and cool the entire home. Instead, take the time to close off areas you are not using. You will save substantial money on your utilities.

- Use a programmable thermostat: Setting your thermostat to automatically adjust the temperature when you're not at home can help you save money on heating and cooling costs.

- Seal air leaks: Check for leaks around windows, doors, and other areas and seal them to prevent drafts and keep cool air in the summer and warm air in the winter.

- Insulate your home: Proper insulation can help keep your home warm in the winter and cool in the summer, reducing your heating and cooling costs.

- Replace your HVAC filter regularly: A dirty HVAC filter can reduce the efficiency of your heating and cooling system and increase energy costs. Replacing the filter regularly can help keep your system running smoothly.

- Use ceiling fans: Ceiling fans can help circulate air and make your home feel more comfortable, reducing the need for heating and cooling.

- Switch to energy-efficient lighting: Replacing incandescent light bulbs with LED light bulbs can reduce energy costs and help you save money on heating and cooling.

- Invest in energy-efficient appliances: Energy-efficient appliances, such as refrigerators, washers, and dryers, can help reduce energy costs and save money on heating and cooling.

- Plant trees or install shading devices: Planting trees or installing shading devices, such as shading screens or awnings, can help reduce the amount of heat that enters your home and reduce your need for cooling.

- Use window coverings: Closing blinds, curtains, or shades during the day can help reduce the heat that enters your home and reduce your need for cooling. Similarly, keeping them open during the day in the winter can allow the sun to warm your home naturally.

- Service your HVAC system regularly: Regular maintenance and service of your heating and cooling system can help keep it running efficiently and reduce energy costs.

CHAPTER SIX

REALITY OF HEALTHCARE EXPENSES

STRATEGIES FOR SAVING MONEY ON MEDICAL COSTS

I once met a retired couple, Mary and John, who had a telling anecdote about the costs of healthcare in retirement. Mary and John had been married for over 50 years and had saved diligently for their retirement. They had a comfortable nest egg, but were shocked to discover just how much of their savings were being consumed by healthcare costs.

Mary had developed a chronic condition that required regular medication and doctor visits, and the costs quickly added up. They had purchased a comprehensive health insurance plan, but even with insurance, the out-of-pocket expenses were substantial. John was also experiencing some health issues, and the costs of his care were also adding up.

Despite their careful planning and savings, Mary and John found that their healthcare costs were taking a significant bite out of their retirement funds. As a result, they were forced to make difficult choices, such as cutting back on travel and other leisure activities, to ensure they could afford their healthcare needs.

This anecdote highlights just how important it is to plan for healthcare costs in retirement. Mary and John's story serves as a reminder of the importance of considering healthcare costs when planning for retirement and the importance of researching and choosing a comprehensive health insurance plan that meets one's needs and budget.

SAVE ON HEALTHCARE COSTS

Retirees can save on healthcare costs by implementing the following strategies:

- Stay active and engaged.

Maintaining an active and engaged lifestyle can provide physical, mental, and social benefits, helping to maximize your overall well-being.

- Consider a health savings account (HSA). An HSA can provide tax benefits and help pay for healthcare expenses in retirement.

- Tax Advantages: Contributions to an HSA are tax-deductible, and withdrawals used for qualified medical expenses are tax-free.

- Savings: HSAs allow retirees to save money for future medical expenses and potentially lower healthcare costs.

- Portability: HSAs are portable, meaning the funds and the account can be taken with the retiree if they change insurance plans or employers.

- Investment Opportunities: Some HSAs offer investment options, allowing retirees to earn investment income on their savings.

- Coverage for Medicare Costs: Withdrawals from an HSA can be used to pay for Medicare premiums and out-of-pocket expenses not covered by Medicare, such as deductibles, co-payments, and co-insurance.

- It's important to note that while HSAs can be a great savings tool, they also require that retirees have enough funds set aside to cover their high deductible in a medical emergency. Before enrolling in an HSA, retirees should carefully consider their overall financial situation and healthcare needs.

TAKE ADVANTAGE OF MEDICARE

Take advantage of all the benefits offered by Medicare, such as preventive services, which are covered at no cost to beneficiaries.

- Annual wellness visits: Medicare

covers an annual wellness visit to create or update a personalized prevention plan and discuss any health concerns.

- Cancer screenings: Medicare covers several cancer screenings, including mammograms, Pap tests, and colonoscopies.

- Flu and pneumococcal shots: Medicare covers flu and pneumococcal shots to help prevent the flu and pneumonia.

- Bone density tests: Medicare covers bone density tests for beneficiaries at risk of osteoporosis.

- Cardiovascular screenings:

Medicare covers several cardiovascular screenings, such as cholesterol tests and electrocardiograms.

- Diabetes screenings: Medicare covers diabetes screenings for beneficiaries with risk factors or symptoms.

- Depression screenings: Medicare covers depression screenings for beneficiaries with depression symptoms.

- Glaucoma tests: Medicare covers glaucoma tests for beneficiaries at high risk of the disease.

It's important to note that while Medicare covers these preventative services, some services may have associated costs, such as deductibles or coinsurance. Beneficiaries should check with their Medicare plan to understand their specific coverage and cost-sharing responsibilities.

USE MEDICARE SUPPLEMENT PLANS

Consider purchasing a Medicare Supplement plan to help cover out-of-pocket costs, such as deductibles and copayments.

COMPARE COSTS

Shop around and compare costs for health services, such as prescription drugs, medical procedures, and durable medical equipment, to find the best prices.

Know your coverage: Before you start shopping around, make sure you understand your insurance coverage and what your plan covers and does not cover.

- Use online cost comparison tools: Websites such as Medicare's Plan Finder and private healthcare cost comparison sites can provide an estimate of costs for different procedures, drugs, and medical equipment.

- Check with your healthcare provider: Your healthcare provider may be able to provide information on the costs of services, procedures, or treatments you need and help you compare costs with other providers.

- Consider generic options: If you need a prescription drug, consider asking your doctor if a generic version is available. Generic drugs can often be significantly less expensive than their brand-name counterparts.

- Shop around for durable medical equipment: If you need durable medical equipment, such as a wheelchair or walker, shop around and compare prices at different retailers.

- Negotiate costs: Don't be afraid to negotiate the cost of services with your healthcare provider or supplier. Some providers may be willing to lower their fees to compete for your business.

- Use your HSA or FSA: If you have a Health Savings Account (HSA) or Flexible Spending Account (FSA), you can use these accounts to pay for eligible medical expenses, potentially lowering your overall costs.

- It's important to keep in mind that cost should not be the only factor considered when making decisions about your healthcare. Quality of care, convenience, and expertise of the provider should also be taken into account when making a decision.

USE GENERIC DRUGS AND DISCOUNTS

Consider using generic drugs instead of brand-name drugs, as they can be significantly less expensive. Take advantage of discounts offered by prescription drug programs, such as the Medicare Part D Low-Income Subsidy (LIS) program, to reduce the cost of prescription drugs.

STAY HEALTHY

Adopting healthy lifestyle habits, such as exercising regularly and eating a balanced diet, can help reduce the risk of developing chronic health conditions that can be expensive to treat.

USE COMMUNITY RESOURCES

Take advantage of community resources, such as senior centers and local programs, that offer health and wellness services at no or low cost.

CONSIDER LONG-TERM CARE INSURANCE

Consider purchasing long-term care insurance to help cover the cost of long-term care services, such as home health care, nursing home care, or assisted living.

GET ANOTHER OPINION

Consider getting a second opinion before undergoing a major medical procedure, as this can help ensure that the procedure is necessary and the cost is reasonable.

SAVE ON VET BILLS

Being a pet owner is a joy for many reasons, but one of my most memorable experiences was adopting my first rescue dog. Kev was shy and timid when I first brought her home, but with patience and love, she blossomed into a happy, playful, and affectionate companion. She would always greet me with wagging tail and licks, and she would snuggle up with me on the couch when I needed some comfort. Kev also taught me the importance of responsibility and the joy of giving back, as I trained her and provided her with the care she needed. Whether we were taking walks in the park, playing fetch, or just cuddling, every moment with Kevwas a source of happiness and unconditional love.

Pets are considered a family member by many and there are ways to save on veterinary bills:

- Regular check-ups and preventive care: Regular check-ups and preventive care, such as vaccinations and flea treatments, can help prevent more costly medical problems in the future.

- Pet insurance: Consider purchasing pet insurance to help cover unexpected veterinary bills.

- Shop around: Compare prices at different veterinary clinics to find one that fits your budget.

- Ask about payment plans: Some veterinary clinics offer payment plans or financing options to help manage the cost of care.

- Negotiate costs: Be bold and ask for discounts or negotiate fees for veterinary services.

- Stock up on supplies: Bulk buying supplies, such as food and medication, can save money.

- Consider alternative treatments: Ask your veterinarian about alternative therapies, such as herbal remedies or acupuncture, which may be less expensive than traditional medical treatments.

- Consider pet-friendly housing: Renting a pet-friendly apartment or living in a community with a dog park can help reduce the need for expensive pet services, such as boarding or dog walking.

- Take advantage of free resources: Utilize free resources, such as online pet health forums or local pet groups, for advice and support.

Note: Always prioritize your pet's health and well-being, and never skimp on veterinary care if needed. Consult your veterinarian for personalized advice on how to save on veterinary bills for your pet's specific needs.

HOME REMEDIES

Before rushing off to see the doctor for a sore throat, try some home remedies or over-the-counter drugs instead. For a sore throat, butter mixed with ginger and sugar makes a soothing healing pate. A hot toddy before bed is great for a cold.

Ask your family for their home remedies and try them. Sometimes a simple over-the-counter medication or herb will do the trick without costing you an expensive doctor's office visit.

- Headache: Apply a cold compress to the forehead or massage the temples to relieve headache pain.

- Sore throat: Gargle with salt water or sip warm tea with honey and lemon to soothe a sore throat.

- Cough: Drink warm liquids, such as tea with honey or soup, to help relieve coughing.

- Nausea: Ginger, such as in the form of tea or candies, can help relieve nausea.

- Indigestion: Drink peppermint tea or chew on a peppermint leaf to help ease indigestion.

- Insomnia: Practice relaxation techniques such as deep breathing or meditation to help improve sleep.

- Allergies: Use a saline nasal rinse or take an antihistamine to relieve allergy symptoms.

- Cold or flu: Stay hydrated with water and other fluids, and rest as much as possible to help your body recover from a cold or flu.

- Muscle pain: Apply a warm compress or take a warm bath to help relieve muscle pain.

- Sunburn: Apply aloe vera gel or cool compresses to the affected area to soothe sunburned skin.

Note: These remedies are not a substitute for professional medical treatment, and it's always best to consult a doctor if you have a severe or persistent ailment.

CHALLENGE THE DOCTOR/ HOSPITAL

If you have stayed in the hospital recently, you know the outrageous charges associated with everything used. For example, while you could buy a box of bandages for a small cut in the drugstore for $5.00, at the hospital, they will charge you $25 for one bandage.

While the government and insurance companies are cracking down on these charges, you should check things closely and challenge anything that is ridiculously priced.

The same is true for your doctor. For example, one woman having a hysterectomy was asked by her doctor if she wanted her appendix removed simultaneously.

The patient thought it was a good idea and agreed. However, after the surgery, when the bill came, there was an additional $3,200 for removing the appendix, although the doctor never mentioned an extra charge. The woman called her doctor to discuss this, and the doctor removed the charge. If something seems way out of balance, question it.

Something else that most people do not know about is what is called "professional courtesy." If you are having financial difficulties, you can ask your doctor if they will write off any balance owed as a professional courtesy. Many will, and if not, the total amount, at least some.

GOOD HEALTH

You need to make sure you take care of yourself physically. For example, missed dental cleanings (every six months) can lead to gum disease or tooth decay that can cost thousands to fix.

The same is true for your health. After trying home remedies or over-the-counter medications, if you still do not feel well, see a doctor. It is far better to pay the doctor's visit than to let your simple summer cold turn into pneumonia.

- Exercise regularly: Aim for at least 30 minutes of physical activity every day. This can include walking, swimming, or doing yoga.

- Eat a balanced diet: Include plenty of fruits, vegetables, whole

grains, and lean proteins. Limit
your intake of sugar, salt, and
saturated fat.

- Stay hydrated: Drink plenty of
water and limit your intake of
sugary drinks.

- Get adequate sleep: Aim for 7-8
hours per night.

- Manage stress: Practice relaxation
techniques, such as meditation or
deep breathing.

- Keep your mind active: Engage
in activities that challenge your
brain, such as reading, solving
puzzles, or learning a new skill.

- Stay connected: Maintain social

connections with friends and family, and consider joining a social group or club.

- Get regular check-ups: Schedule regular appointments with your doctor to monitor your health and address any issues promptly.

- Avoid smoking and limit alcohol consumption: Smoking and excessive alcohol consumption can have serious health consequences.

- Take care of your mental health: Seek help if you are experiencing symptoms of depression or anxiety.

SQUELCH THE SMOKING

This is probably the most problematic habit to break. Still, in addition to saving your health, you will also save money. Cigarettes have become quite expensive, and if you can quit smoking, you will enjoy breathing easier and having more to put away for a rainy day.

CHAPTER SEVEN

RELAX FRUGAL TRAVEL

TIPS FOR ENJOYING LIFE WITHOUT BREAKING THE BANK

Tom and Mary loved to travel. They had always dreamed of seeing the world and were eager to make the most of their retirement years. However, they were also careful with their finances and didn't want to spend all their savings on travel.

One day, Tom and Mary stumbled upon a group of travelers who lived frugally and had found ways to enjoy their travels without breaking the bank. They learned the importance of budgeting, public transportation, staying in affordable accommodations, and eating like locals. They also discovered the joy of slow travel, where they could spend more time in one place and get to know the local culture.

Tom and Mary were inspired by these tips and decided to put them into practice on their next trip. They found that by traveling more slowly and mindfully, they could experience a new country and its culture in a much deeper way. They also discovered they could save money on food by cooking their meals or eating at local markets and street vendors.

Ultimately, Tom and Mary learned they could travel the world without breaking the bank. They could see incredible sights, meet fascinating people, and enjoy new cultures without sacrificing their savings. They realized that by being mindful and creative, they could have the trips of a lifetime and still have enough money to enjoy their retirement years. They learned that with some planning and flexibility, they could have the time of their lives without sacrificing their financial security.

PLAN IN ADVACE

Booking your travel well in advance can often result in lower prices for flights, accommodations, and activities.

COMPARE PRICES

Shop around and compare prices from different airlines, hotels, and travel websites to find the best deal. Look for package deals: Consider purchasing a package vacation deal that includes flights, hotels, and activities for a discounted rate.

BE FLEXIBLE

Being flexible with your travel dates and destination can often result in lower prices. While Paris, England, or Germany offers excitement, they also cost money to visit. Unfortunately, people regularly need to remember the

United States and even the state where they live.

One man had lived in Arizona his entire life. At age 50, when asked by a friend what the Grand Canyon was like, he was unable to answer because he had never been there.

The next time you get ready to plan your vacation, look around where you live and consider an exciting road trip that will not only be educational but cost-effective. A vacation does not have to be expensive to be fun and memorable.

USE REWARD PROGRAMS

Take advantage of rewards programs offered by airlines, hotels, and credit cards to earn points or miles that can be redeemed for free or discounted travel.

PACK SMART

Bring only what you need and pack light to save on baggage fees. Here are some tips to pack for a

10-day trip using only a carry-on bag:

- Make a packing list: Start by making a list of everything you need to bring. This will help you avoid overpacking and ensure you don't forget any essential items.

- Choose versatile clothing: Pack clothing that can be mixed and matched to create different outfits. Stick to basic colors and classic styles that can be dressed up or down. This will help you maximize your outfit options while minimizing the number of items you need to pack.

- Roll your clothes: Rolling your clothes instead of folding them can help you save space in your bag. Plus, it can help prevent wrinkles.

- Use packing cubes: Packing cubes are a great way to stay organized and make the most of the space in your bag. Use them to group items like socks, underwear, and toiletries together.

- Wear your bulkiest items: If you're traveling with bulky items like a winter coat or boots, wear them on the plane to save space in your bag.

- Pack travel-sized toiletries: To save space, pack travel-sized toiletries or transfer your favorite products into smaller containers.

- Consider doing laundry: If you're going to be away for 10 days, you may need to do laundry at some point. Plan to do laundry at your destination, or pack a small amount of laundry detergent so you can wash clothes in your hotel sink.

- Be strategic with your personal item: In addition to your carry-on bag, you may be allowed to bring a personal item like a purse or backpack. Use this space to pack items like your laptop, book, or snacks.

By following these tips, you should be able to pack everything you need for a 10-day trip in a carry-on bag.

EAT IN

Eat at local restaurants or cooking your meals instead of dining out can save a lot of money on food expenses.

USE PUBLIC TRANSIT

Use public transportation: Using public transportation instead of taxis, or rental cars can save money and provide a unique cultural experience.

AVOID PEAK SEASON

Traveling during off-peak seasons can lower flights and accommodation prices. Generally, airfare, hotel, and car prices are substantially lower than traveling during peak times. If you look at all your options, you can come close to the date you would like to travel. For example, flying to Hawaii through June 8 is considered off-season, while June 9 is the peak. One day makes a massive price difference.

RESEARCH FREE THINGS TO DO

Research and take advantage of free activities and events in your destination, such as festivals, museums, or parks.

By following these tips, you can save money on travel and have more resources available for other aspects of your trip.

CHAPTER EIGHT

RECHARGE

STAYING ACTIVE AND ENGAGED

FINDING AFFORDABLE HOBBIES AND INTERESTS

If you are tired of being bored, you will be pleased to learn that there are hundreds of things to do that do not cost a dime. For example, if you want a little Friday or Saturday night excitement, sign up at your local police department for a "ride-a-long" where you can go on duty with an officer as they respond to actual calls.

In addition, community colleges always offer free exercise classes, and coffee shops have poetry readings.

Entertainment and having fun do not have to cost anything. Some cities have special areas popular on the weekends where you can find free concerts. Check your local paper and college to get a list for your area. Local parks and nature areas: Many local parks and nature areas offer free activities such as hiking, picnicking, and wildlife watching.

COMMUNITY EVENTS

Check your local community calendar for free events such as festivals, concerts, and street fairs.

OUTDOOR ACTIVITIES

Gardening is a popular outdoor activity that can be both relaxing and productive. You can start with a small herb or vegetable garden in your backyard and watch your plants grow. Hiking, bird watching, and camping are also outdoor activities that can be enjoyed without breaking the bank. You can find local parks or hiking trails that are free or low-cost, and camping equipment can be rented or borrowed.

ARTS AND CRAFTS

Arts and crafts such as painting, drawing, knitting, and scrapbooking are low-cost hobbies that can be enjoyed at home. You can purchase supplies at local discount or dollar stores, or you can use household items like paper, pencils, or yarn. You can also join a local arts and crafts group to meet others who share your interests and learn new techniques.

VOLUNTEERING

Many organizations rely on volunteers, and volunteering can be a fulfilling and low-cost way to spend your time. You can search for opportunities in your community or online, and choose an organization that aligns with your interests and skills. Some examples of volunteer opportunities include working with animals, helping at a food bank, or tutoring students.

READING AND WRITING

If you enjoy reading or writing, you can join a local book club, start a blog, or become a member of a library. Libraries often have a wide selection of books and magazines available for free, and many offer workshops and classes on writing and other topics.

LEARNING A NEW SKILL

You can take advantage of free or low-cost classes offered by community organizations, libraries, or adult education programs to learn a new skill. Classes may include cooking, photography, or computer skills. You can also use online resources, such as YouTube tutorials or online courses, to learn a new skill.

PLAYING GAMES

Playing board games, cards, or video games can be a fun and low-cost way to spend your time. You can borrow games from a library, play with friends, or purchase used games at a low cost.

SOCIALIZING

Spending time with friends and family can be an affordable way to enjoy your time. You can plan a picnic, have a movie night, or attend local events and activities. You can also join a social club to meet new people and participate in group activities. Many clubs offer memberships for a low cost or for free.

GEOCACHING

Geocaching is a treasure-hunting game that involves using GPS to find hidden containers. It can be a fun and challenging outdoor activity that can be enjoyed alone or with friends.

GENEALOGY

Genealogy research - Researching your family history can be a fascinating and rewarding hobby that can be done online or at local libraries and archives.

BOOKBINDING

Bookbinding - Seniors who enjoy reading may also enjoy learning how to bind their own books. There are many instructional videos and tutorials available online, and basic bookbinding supplies can be purchased inexpensively.

ART

Painting or drawing en plein air - Seniors who enjoy art may want to try painting or drawing outdoors. All that's needed is some basic art supplies and a scenic location.

VIRTUAL TRAVEL

Virtual travel - Seniors who are unable to travel may enjoy exploring the world from the comfort of their own home through virtual travel experiences. Many museums, galleries, and tourist attractions offer virtual tours and experiences.

WRITING

Writing memoirs - Writing memoirs can be a meaningful and fulfilling activity for seniors who want to share their life experiences and memories with loved ones.

If you're interested in learning more about this topic, I have written a more comprehensive book titled Beyond Bingo 100 Things to do During Retirement which, provides even more in-depth information and practical tips. It covers topics such as how to rewire, reconnect, relax, and reclaim with bits of trivia and anecdotes from me. For those who want to delve deeper into this subject, this book is highly recommended.

In conclusion, there are countless ways to have fun and enjoy life without spending a lot of money. From participating in free community events and outdoor activities, to pursuing low-cost hobbies like arts and crafts, reading, and playing games, there are options for everyone. Additionally, volunteering and learning new skills can be both fulfilling and enriching experiences. By taking advantage of these opportunities, you can fill your free time with enjoyable and meaningful activities without breaking the bank. So next time you're feeling bored, remember that there are plenty of low-cost options available to you.

Reflect

Final words embracing a fulfilling and frugal retirement lifestyle

In conclusion, embracing a fulfilling and money-saving retirement lifestyle is the key to a comfortable and secure future. By making smart financial decisions and living within your means, you can ensure that you have enough resources to enjoy your golden years to the fullest. Whether you're downsizing your home, finding ways to save on groceries and household expenses, or pursuing new hobbies and interests, there are countless opportunities to live frugally and make the most of your retirement years. The important thing is to have a plan, stay focused, and be flexible. Doing so lets you can enjoy a fulfilling and money-saving retirement, filled with adventures, joy, and peace of mind. So embrace a frugal and fulfilling retirement lifestyle, and make the most of your golden years.

The book provides a comprehensive guide to help individuals take control of their finances in retirement. By addressing the different aspects of retirement finances, the book offers a comprehensive solution to financial planning in retirement. The chapters in the book are carefully crafted to provide readers with the necessary information and tools to make informed decisions about their finances.

For example, by realizing their current financial situation and reassessing their spending habits, readers can identify areas where they can make changes to reduce their expenses. The strategies for reducing expenditures on groceries and household items and rebalancing their retirement income provide readers with practical tips to make their money go further. Additionally, the book covers the realities of healthcare expenses and offers strategies for saving money on medical costs, which can be a significant expense in retirement.

Moreover, the book provides options for reducing housing costs and finding affordable hobbies and interests to keep readers engaged and active. This helps to ensure that they can live a fulfilling retirement without breaking the bank.

In conclusion, the book is a valuable resource for individuals seeking to take control of their finances in retirement. By following the strategies outlined in the book, readers can enjoy a secure and fulfilling retirement, free from financial worries. The book provides a comprehensive approach to financial planning in retirement, ensuring that readers are well-equipped to face the challenges ahead.

JUST FOR YOU!

A FREE GIFT TO OUR READERS

Join the Retirement Ready Facebook Group for
free printable templates and checklists to start
your retirement journey right away!
Scan the QR code or vist this link:

https://www.facebook.com/groups/514793100830900

LEAVE A 1-CLICK REVIEW!

I would be incredibly thankful if you could take just 60 seconds to write a brief review on Amazon, even if it is just a few sentences!

Click here to leave a quick review

About the Author

June Dashlane

June is a highly respected time management coach and certified organization expert. With her busy schedule and growing demand for her expertise in the retirement niche, she has created the "Retirement Ready"

series of books to help others smoothly transition to their next chapter in life.

As a seasoned professional, June has the unique ability to take the complexities of retirement planning and break them down into simple, easy-to-follow steps. When she's not busy helping clients achieve their goals, June enjoys the simple life on her farm in Wisconsin, surrounded by her pets and chickens. Her passion for helping others and her expertise in the retirement field make her the go-to expert for anyone looking to retire with confidence and ease.

OTHER BOOKS YOU'LL LOVE

RETIREMENT READY SERIES

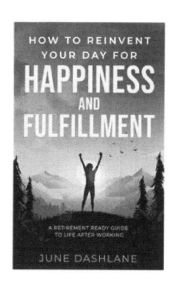

AVAILABLE ON AMAZON:
https://www.amazon.com/s?k=June+Da
shlane&i=digital-text&ref=nb_sb_noss

OTHER BOOKS YOU'LL LOVE

RETIREMENT READY SERIES

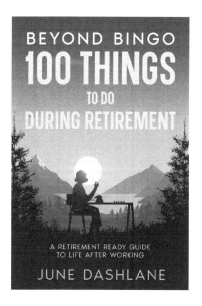

AVAILABLE ON AMAZON:
https://www.amazon.com/s?k=June+Da
shlane&i=digital-text&ref=nb_sb_noss

REFERENCES

https://armyresidence.com/blog/the-ea
gle/helpful-tips-downsizing-retirement?
gclid=Cj0KCQiA9YugBhCZARIsAACXxeL
RsOYJT4VSvUlt9RO-XhkPlFQ3xt-54v2dc
7RtnQSh7vYjuDVbm5YaAjlMEALw_wcB

https://www.cleartrip.com/collections/l
ong-trip-packing-planning-tips/#:~:text=
FAQs,of%20a%20few%20miscellaneous
%20accessories.

https://evernote.com/blog/how-to-mak
e-a-grocery-list/

www.fidelity.com

https://www.investopedia.com/health-savings-account-hsa-4775648

https://www.thebalance.com/how-downsizing-can-save-you-money-4164394

www.medicare.gov

Illustrations designed by Sarah Moran